# KING OF THE
# MOUNTAINS

## The Remarkable Story of
## Giuseppe Musolino,
## Italy's Most Famous Outlaw

# Dan Possumato

**Smoky City Press**
Pittsburgh, PA

## Praise for King of the Mountains

*"A gripping account of an Italian peasant accused of a crime he didn't commit...[a] well-written tale."*

-Tony Norman,
**Pittsburgh Post-Gazette**

*"...well researched...easy to read...a factual account of this intriguing slice of Calabrian history"*

-Sarah Mastroianni,
**Panoram Italia**, Toronto

*"[An] electrifying true tale, which at times reads like the strangest fiction"*

-**Italian American Digest**,
New Orleans

*"Considered by historians as either "Italy's Robin Hood" or a depraved assassin, this well-researched book lets you decide."*

-**Ambassador Magazine**,
National Italian American Foundation

Copyright © 2013 by Daniel P. Possumato

All rights reserved worldwide. No part of this book may be reproduced or transmitted in any form or by any means without written permission from the author, except in the case of brief quotations embodied in critical articles and reviews.

Smoky City Press
213 Emerson Avenue
Pittsburgh, PA 15215
Tel 503-951-8456

Book Design: Amy Pogue

Library of Congress Cataloging-in-Publication Data:

*Possumato, Dan*

*King of the Mountains: The Remarkable Story of Giuseppe Musolino, Italy's Most Famous Outlaw, 1st ed.*

*ISBN 978-0-615-78684-1*

*1. Biography 2. Criminals & Outlaws 3. History*

First edition paperback: March 2013

1 2 3 4 5 6 7 8 9 10

Printed in the United States of America

*For Giovanni, Vittoria and Fortunata Musolino, my grandparents and mother who emigrated from Italy to America, and from whom I first heard the stories of our relative Giuseppe.*

# Contents

# Preface

"He was the Robin Hood of Italy," my mother said when she first showed me the tattered old book in Italian that she kept in her cedar chest. I was immediately interested because I was an avid follower of the immensely popular 1950's TV series *The Adventures of Robin Hood.* The book was the story of Giuseppe Musolino, whose last name was the same as the maiden name of my mother. As I thumbed through the pages I stopped at an illustration showing a man in a prison uniform breaking rocks with a sledgehammer. He wore an iron ankle shackle with a short length of chain attached to a heavy ball, just like I had seen in a few silent movies. This was the Mediterranean version of the gallant hero of Sherwood Forest? "If he was a hero, why does this drawing show him in prison?" I asked.

I was told his story was "complicated," and indeed it is. It is a tale of what happened when a harsh injustice was imposed by the government upon an innocent man, provoking him to commit injustices himself.

In conducting research for this manuscript I encountered dozens of primary source materials that indicated an astounding number of contradictions regarding dates, locations, circumstances, numbers and even names of Musolino's victims. In most cases I have chosen to include information that was substantiated by at least two independent sources, but this was not always possible.

Although there have been over a dozen books about Giuseppe Musolino written in Italian, this is the first available in English. I have sought to bring together in one source the main points of his incredible story, one that still is well known in Italy today.

I discovered this a few years ago when I was working temporarily at an Italian army base near Pisa. I was part of a training team conducting an exercise with the American and Italian forces stationed there, which included some members of the Carabinieri, Italy's famous national police force organized as a military unit. During a break I joked with one of them that his organization used to chase after a relative of mine, my grandfather's first cousin. The officer was genuinely intrigued, and he told me the Musolino affair is still mentioned in their academy's curriculum. After lunch I was surprised to suddenly find myself surrounded by six or seven smiling Carabinieri, who wanted to have a group picture taken with a relative of Musolino. Even today, over one hundred eleven years after his trial, the name of Giuseppe Musolino has not faded from the Italian collective memory.

I wish to acknowledge the assistance of the Reference Services Department of the Carnegie Library of Pittsburgh, whose outstanding physical collection of periodicals and newspapers enabled me to read contemporary accounts of Musolino's exploits as reported in the original domestic and foreign publications.

I also wish to thank my wife, Ellen Steinbart, for her willingness to review my manuscript and her kind offerings of sound advice for editing.

Dan Possumato
Pittsburgh
March 16, 2013

Giuseppe Musolino

# Introduction

*"The King of the Mountains is locked in jail, and he
too dreams of the beloved land."*

-Italian folk song referring to Musolino

SO BEGAN A 1956 TIME MAGAZINE ARTICLE noting the
death of Giuseppe Musolino* in January of that year.[1]
Nearly sixty years earlier Musolino had been dubbed "King
of the Mountains" by the Italian press, and his exploits had
been front-page news around the world. The article went
on to say, "Few soldiers of fortune before or since have
become so legendary in so short a time."

Regarded by many Italians as "The Robin Hood of
Italy," Giuseppe Musolino is dismissed by others as a
cunning yet depraved and remorseless assassin. The drama
surrounding Musolino's life at the turn of the 20th century
was well-reported at the time in the major news publications of Europe and the United States. While many of these

---

*Although their surnames are similar, he is not to be confused with the
Fascist dictator Benito Mussolini.

accounts contain half-truths, erroneous and one suspects invented information, there is a short list of specifics that are generally acknowledged to be historically accurate.

Giuseppe Musolino was born on September 24, 1876, in the isolated hill town of Santo Stefano d'Aspromonte in southern Italy's province of Calabria. He was of peasant birth, although he claimed to be descended from French nobility. He worked as a woodcutter and carpenter, and he was an occasional helper in his father's wine shop. In the year 1897, at age 21, he was accused of the attempted murder of a political -and some say also romantic -rival. Although he maintained his innocence at the time and for the remainder of his life, he was convicted of the crime and sentenced to 21 years at hard labor. At the conclusion of the trial Musolino swore vengeance upon those who had falsely accused him, testified against him, and convicted him. He vowed to escape and murder them all, including the prosecuting attorney and the judge. It was seen as just another hollow threat made by a newly-condemned man.

It proved not to be an idle one. Less than four months later Giuseppe Musolino did indeed escape, along with three other inmates from the supposedly airtight prison at Gerace Marina, present day Locri. For the next three years he eluded a massive manhunt conducted by not only the police but also by the Italian army. He largely fulfilled his vendetta, although the number of people he killed has never been precisely determined. The lowest reported figure was 9, the highest 25, with 19 as the most often cited. He became a hero to the vast majority of the common people who inhabited the poverty-stricken region of Italy's far south, although he also had many admirers from among the wealthy. In the mass psyche he quickly evolved into a secular equivalent of David, doing battle with the Goliath of a corrupt judicial system. Many of the local inhabitants provided him with supplies, information and shelter which enabled him to roam free and evade his pursuers for years. Musolino was eventually apprehended, tried anew, and returned to prison. In 1946 he was pronounced insane[2] and transferred to a mental institution in Reggio di Calabria. He died at age 80 after spending more than 54 years in confinement.

Let there be no doubt that he was famous while his legend was in the making and for many years beyond, roughly from 1899 to the 1930's. In 1901 America's ranking magazines of news and opinions were *The Independent, The Nation,* and *The Outlook.* All three published multiple stories about Musolino, as did many other publications such as the *Los Angeles Times, The Washington Post, The New York Times, The Boston Daily Globe* (now *The Boston Globe*), *The Times of London* and many other newspapers around the world. There have been two films made of his life, one in the silent era and one in the 1950's, but no copies of them are known to have survived.

Giuseppe Musolino, or "Beppe" or "Peppino," as he was called, once made world news headlines. Not only was he the undisputed hero of southern Italy, but he also intrigued many around the globe with his defiance of an entire government in order to proclaim his innocence and seek his revenge. However you finally decide to think of him – hero, rogue, or someone in-between – his story is one unique in the annals of outlaws.

# The Making of an Outlaw

*"Ages of oppression and misrule have passed over their heads; sun and rain, with all their caprice, have been kinder friends to them than their earthly masters."*

-Norman Douglas, in his book *Old Calabria*

SANTO STEFANO SITS HIGH IN THE MOUNTAINS of Aspromonte, the wildest part of the southern Apennine range, about 400 miles southeast of Rome near the toe of the Italian boot. It is a remote area, but one of spectacular scenic beauty, rich in history and tradition. Roman legions camped there as far back as the second century BC, during the wars with Carthage. Most towns in the area were built after the fall of the Roman Empire specifically because their isolation afforded a manner of security, as the empire's collapse had exposed the region's coastal settlements to frequent raids by a host of plunderers. It was in these mountains, in 1862, where Garibaldi's Red Shirts suffered defeat at the Battle of Aspromonte.[3] Today Santo Stefano's population numbers less than 1400, reduced by the great migrations that occurred during the first half of the 20th century. However, in 1897 the town boasted a population of around 3000. It is located about 18 miles from the provincial capital of Reggio di Calabria, but the road winding up through the mountains to the town, elevation 2346 feet, was formidable for the horse drawn wagons and carriages of that era. Santo Stefano was, in more ways than one, a world apart from the more developed areas of Italy.

H.D. Sedgwick, Jr., writing for *The Outlook* in 1902, summarized the conditions that explain very well the circumstances which existed at the time of Musolino.

> "The southern end of Calabria is naturally rich, but the land has been greatly neglected. Crops are ignorantly cultivated and badly harvested. Olives, for instance, are allowed to stay on the trees till they rot, so that the oil is worthless except for soap. There is no proper irrigation, and therefore no supply of water; cattle die by scores, and cows give no milk. The trees in the forests are recklessly cut and burned. Moreover, the government has been bad for hundreds of years. It has encouraged large holdings by the great landlords, who, deeming good husbandry incompatible with their aristocratic customs, have suffered the land to deteriorate, and have let the peasants, who ought to have been a class of peasant proprietors, degenerate into a poverty-stricken tenantry. The great landlords have been tyrants on their domains, administering injustice as they pleased. It has been said that the explanation of the admiration which the

people entertain for the brigands lies in the tyranny of the rich over the poor; the peasants enjoy seeing the brigands maltreat their tyrants, and do not fear robbers themselves, for they have nothing that can be stolen." [4]

Not much is known about Musolino's youth, although several sources attest to him having had trouble with the law. He is reported to have accidentally killed a companion during an argument when he was only eleven and subsequently served some time in jail for this act. At the age of fifteen he threatened his father so convincingly that the older Musolino sought protection from the Carabinieri.* Yet Giuseppe was regarded as a good orator, a cultivated writer, and somewhat of a handsome rake with the ladies. His favorite book was "*The Thousand and One Nights*," [5] and from an early age he was known to have possessed political ambitions.

On October 27, 1897 Musolino became involved in a violent quarrel with one Vincenzo Zoccoli at the tavern Osteria della Frasca. Both men were competing for leadership of the local branch of the "*picciotteria*," a society with political overtones based on secrecy, camaraderie, honor, and if necessary, violence. [6] The two were, however, at opposite ends of the social scale, as the Zoccolis were among the most prosperous and influential families in town, while Musolino's family was of more modest means. A full-scale

---

* The Carabinieri were, and are, the national paramilitary police of Italy. The term was often used interchangeably with the word "soldiers" in press reports of the day, although the two forces were in fact distinct from one another.

brawl broke out and spilled into the street, which also drew in some of the other men who had been present. Out came the ubiquitous Calabrian knives with blades almost a foot long. "The struggle would have continued if the partisans of both had not arrived on the spot, exchanging revolver shots and separating the two."[7] Whether the origin of the hostility was about politics or a woman is uncertain, but in the end Zoccoli had stabbed his adversary in the hands and arms over 40 times.[8]

Musolino was taken to the house of his parents so that his wounds could be treated. He was put into bed where he lay for several days, and it was far from certain that he would fully recover.

Two days after the altercation Zoccoli was himself shot by an unknown marksman. The most popular account held that the assailant had fired from behind a wall or fence, and therefore had remained unseen. Zoccoli was wounded but survived.

His family went to the police and made a statement claiming they had witnesses who had heard the would-be assassin shout out immediately after the shooting "Are you dead, scoundrel?" and had recognized the voice as Musolino's.[9] They also alleged that his hat was found near the scene and that he had sworn a vendetta against their family. One version of what happened next is that Musolino could not even get out of bed without assistance, and he was soon arrested by the local police and carried to the town jail on a litter. Another account had the police taking a long time to decide if charges should be brought, and by the time they decided to arrest him, Musolino had taken flight. He was on the run for six months before he was finally arrested, together with a cousin named Antonio

Filastò, who had been involved in the original brawl. They were found sleeping at the house of Filastò's mother, also Musolino's aunt, who lived in a neighboring village. Considering that Musolino's trial would not be concluded until September of 1898, almost a year after the shooting, this latter version seems more plausible.

Shortly after his apprehension he was arraigned before the district magistrate and transported to Reggio di Calabria to stand trial on charges of attempted murder. He was also charged for publically swearing a vendetta, which in itself was illegal in Italy. In many cases issuing such an oath was seen by southern Italians as an entirely rational response to a transgression, made necessary by the weak and corrupt rule of law in the region. The implication of Musolino's supposed vendetta was fully known: he would hold other members of the Zoccoli family responsible for whatever wrong had been done to him, as if they had themselves committed the alleged offense. "There was great excitement in San Stefano over the affair, most of the people taking the side of Musolino." [10]

The trial, which also included Filastò as a co-conspirator, was presided over by "a notorious protector" [11] of an opposing political faction with which Musolino had often been at odds. In the courtroom the defendants stood or sat in the dock, which was a cell set up to prevent their communication with others, even their own lawyers, as well as to minimize any potential violent outbursts. Most sources relate that the charges against them were based on circumstantial evidence, and there is no doubt that many witnesses committed perjury, if not for money then out of intimidation by the Zoccolis. Musolino was furious with each new piece of evidence brought forward, and often stood up in the dock and shook the bars violently to show his contempt for their testimony. His defense lawyers were not permitted to call several witnesses that would have supported his plea of innocence, which further enraged him. In the end he was sentenced to 21years at hard labor, and Filastò was to serve a 7 year term.[12] As soon as the sentence was pronounced, Filastò's sister collapsed and died on the spot.[13]

Both the guilty verdict and the death of his cousin provoked Musolino to cry out that he had never before declared a vendetta against the Zoccolis, but that he did so now.[14] Livid with rage, he again shook the bars of the dock and shouted that he was innocent and that everyone in the courtroom knew this was true. He scrutinized the chief judge, the prosecutor, and the witnesses and swore that he would never accept imprisonment. "I shall come out and not one traitor will remain!"[15] The room fell silent. Musolino was led out of the dock in handcuffs, and as he was escorted past one of his accusers he gave him a swift kick. Gasps erupted throughout the courtroom. There was good reason to believe that if Musolino were ever to escape, he would make good on his vow of revenge.

Illustrations in Italian magazines published a few years later show Musolino in prison, breaking rocks in the hot Calabrian sun. He wouldn't have to do so for long, as he, Filastò and two other prisoners soon hatched a daring escape plot. The prison at Gerace Marina, a former fortress, was considered to be virtually escape-proof. However, the conspirators discovered that the masonry in one section, possibly their communal cell, had deteriorated from within but had gone unnoticed by the prison authorities. Musolino later said that St. Joseph had come to him in a dream and suggested the exact portion of the wall where they should dig. They secretly constructed a ladder fashioned from bed sheets and slats, the later serving as rungs. Sometime during the night of January 9th, 1899 they broke through the wall, climbed down the makeshift ladder then undertook a frightening 25 foot freefall for the final drop to the ground. His companions were soon recaptured, but Musolino managed to evade his pursuers, and he would continue to do so for almost the next three years. One of the first things he did was to contact a priest to arrange a mass in honor of St. Joseph, to give thanks for the saint having helped him escape.[16]

When news of Musolino's breakout reached Santo Stefano, it was clear that he would now begin extracting revenge upon those whom he believed had wronged him. What wasn't clear was how lethal and terrifying it would be, and how his actions would capture the interest of the province, then the entire country, and ultimately much of Europe and the Americas. It still ranks as one of the most bloody and shocking solo acts of retribution in European history.

Giuseppe Musolino was about to become famous.

# Fulfillment of the Vendetta

*"You must know there are two ways of contesting, the one by the law, the other by force; the first method is proper to men, the second to beasts; but because the first is frequently not sufficient, it is necessary to have recourse to the second."*

-Nicolo Machiavelli, The Prince

MUSOLINO WALKED FOR 20 STRAIGHT HOURS until he succeeded in making his way to the mountains and forests of Aspromonte, not far from Santo Stefano.[17] Aspromonte means "rough mountains," and indeed they are: steep, rocky and foreboding. When Musolino was born, Italy had been a unified country for only 15 years. Calabria had previously been governed as part of the Kingdom of the Two Sicilies, ruled by the Spanish branch of the house of Bourbon. Before that it had been controlled by a host of powers, including the French under Napoleon. No matter who conquered the land, the common people remained impoverished and oppressed. The Calabrians became progressively more discontented and managed to mount several revolts, all brutally crushed by the government. Anyone who challenged a regime that supported the nobility and landed classes to the detriment of the general populace, be they bandit or not, was looked upon as a champion of the people. Beppe Musolino soon became that champion.

Musolino found himself in a region full of wild mountains and thick forests, one that he knew well. To a large extent the local population rendered him support, mostly out of admiration for his boldness, and in some cases, fear. Almost immediately he began tracking down those whom he had sworn to kill, the first victims being the two principal witnesses against him at his trial.

Giuseppe Musolino let it be known that he would add to his list anyone who gave information regarding his whereabouts, or for attempting to capture him for the reward that had recently been placed upon his head. Other disaffected men, some known to Musolino and others not, joined him in his life on the run. A band of Merry Men they were not, but the international press soon started comparing their leader to the mythical Robin Hood.

The entire Zoccoli clan knew that they were among Musolino's prime targets, and the men of the family made a point to always be armed and in the company of trusted individuals. One night Musolino and his followers suddenly showed up at Vincenzo Zoccoli's farmhouse and quickly barricaded or nailed shut all the doors and windows, ensuring escape was not possible. Hearing movement from within they believed Zoccoli and his family were inside. The men set fire to the house from four corners all at once. However, Zoccoli and his family were sleeping elsewhere that night, so the perpetrators only succeeded in roasting some pigs and goats. Out of frustration the men cut the hamstrings of all Zoccoli's cattle and burned his wheat field before returning to their hideout. Musolino continued to pursue Vincenzo Zoccoli, but his terrified intended victim took such precautions that Musolino succeeded only in murdering Vincenzo's brother Henrico.

Musolino's settling of scores at this point expanded beyond the Zoccolis. Less than two weeks after burning Zoccoli's house Musolino stabbed to death a man that had given information regarding his whereabouts to the police. Then "at short intervals he fired at three 'spies,' killing one, and, as he had said, 'warning' the others, by wounding them in the legs." [18]

A particularly gruesome slaying was that of Francesco Marte, a peasant who had betrayed Musolino's location to the police. The fugitive had been very ill, and Marte had been attending to his needs. Thinking that he might be near death, Musolino sent Marte to tell his mother and sister he wished to see them. Marte instead went to the police, but was unaware that he had been stealthily followed by one of Musolino's men. Sick as he was, Musolino's companions relocated him to another site on the mountain and the police were once more foiled.

At harvest time after Musolino had recovered, he had been staking out one of Marte's fields in the hope of catching him. In due course Marte came to work in the field together with three or four other men. Musolino, who was alone and had concealed himself amongst the wheat, jumped up in front of them. Said Musolino of the encounter, "How they blubbered and cringed, and grunted and wept…Marte wrung his hands, rolled on the ground, and kissed my feet to move me to pity. Well, I am not made of stone so I agreed to pardon him – for the time being. Then we had some pears together, my favorite fruit, and I left, boldly turning my back on them, so sure was I that they wouldn't send a bullet after me. Yet as I was walking away, the devil of vengeance crept into my soul. It was stronger than my pity, it triumphed over my generosity." [19]

Afterwards Musolino met up with two of his band, Stefano De Lorenzo and Giovanni Jati, and told them he had second thoughts about his decision not to kill Marte. "Let's kill this dog, lest he make another attempt to destroy us," he said. The men answered "The vengeance is yours… he never tried to harm us." The three finally decided to again corner Marte and all of them would fire their guns at once, and let "the Virgin decide whose bullet shall be his undoing." [20]

This deed they subsequently carried out, but St. Mary could not decide which bullet should kill Marte as they only succeeded in wounding him. Musolino cursed Marte for having the impudence not to die, and, as he laid weeping and begging for time to make his peace with God, Musolino finished him off with his knife. [21]

To say the whole region was terrified of Musolino would not be true. Most people hadn't known him or done anything to offend him, so they had nothing to fear. An article in *The Times of London* offered this insight: "In districts like Sicily and Calabria, where vendetta is still considered by the common people to be the ideal form of social justice, it is easy to understand that a character like Musolino should be surrounded by popular affection and his bloodthirsty ferocity forgotten." [22] In fact the people discounted the trail of carnage he was leaving, preferring to think that those who he had slain had deserved it. People began to write songs about him, one of which appears below and was "repeated everywhere in Calabria." [23]

> *E cu li modi mei e cu li me arti,*
> *Seasso li mura e sbalancu li porte.*
> *E or ache me trovo a chiste parti,*
> *Pe mia la libertà, pe autri la morte.*

> With my ways and with my arts,
> I break the walls and throw open the doors.
> Now that I find myself in these parts,
> There is liberty for me and for others death.

Musolino took exceptional precautions to prevent his recapture. "One precaution he took was to keep two dogs with him in the woods; when he went to sleep at night, one lay at his feet and one five hundred yards in the direction of danger, so that their barking produced the effect of a burglar alarm." [24] Those living in the vicinity where they knew Musolino to be staying were expected to alert him when they observed police searching the area. Farmers would grab their guns and shoot at nonexistent sparrows, dogs were provoked to bark, women would sing songs in a loud voice that would be heard and relayed by others from field to field, alerting the outlaw to scurry away. [25]

Musolino's rampage of violence was now widely known throughout most of Italy, and the police force sent against him was increased to include Carabinieri troops from Reggio di Calabria. Undercover Carabinieri posing as charcoal burners, shepherds or labors would show up in the villages of the region and soon begin asking the locals about the outlaw's whereabouts, seemingly out of innocent curiosity. Their true identities were usually, and laughably, obvious and few gave them any information that proved useful. Musolino became all the more emboldened by the failure of the authorities to apprehend him.

Before long Musolino began to win the support of groups outside the peasant class. There is solid evidence that the wealthy and professional classes were among those who gave him encouragement and assistance (money, food, clothes, weapons, shelter, forewarnings about planned police searches, exchange of letters, etc.). "What seems most strange is that he had also the protection of the rich, whom not only he never molested, but to whom he was of considerable utility, as after he established himself on the peaks of the Sila as King of the Forest he rid the country of common malefactors, so that thefts, fires, aggressions, etc., diminished about 80 per cent. The landowners, finding that one brigand alone protected their property better than the Government with all the police, soldiers and carabineers, were ready to assist him with food and money, which amounted always to much less than what they paid in taxes, and they went so far as to discuss the advisability of a petition to Parliament to pardon the bandit." [26]

By May of 1902 the government of King Vittorio Emanuele III led by Prime Minister Giuseppe Zanardelli had had enough. It had become a laughing stock in the press for its inability to put a stop to one woodcutter's campaign of terror. A full regiment of 500 Carabinieri was sent south for the sole purpose of capturing Musolino, and the number of troops was ultimately increased to roughly double that figure.

Still, the odds against capture remained in Musolino's favor. "It was said that he could count on the sympathy of

140,000 Calabrase against the ever failing attempts of 500 men to recapture him." [27] Details of the whole affair began appearing in leading publications in the rest of Europe, as well as in the United States, Great Britain, Canada, Australia and beyond. The stage was now set for high drama as Italy and an outlaw engaged in a deadly game of cat and mouse.

# Musolino as Benefactor and Daredevil

*"We often do good in order that we may do evil
with impunity."*

-Francois De La Rochefoucauld
(1613 -1680)

WITH ALL THESE DEPICTIONS OF BRUTALITY and murder,
how on earth did Musolino start being compared to the gallant Robin Hood, doer of good and champion of the poor?
He had become greatly indignant when he first learned he
was being referred to in newspapers as "il brigante Musolino," meaning a brigand of the common thief variety.
As his fame increased, he sought to counter this label by
performing acts of magnanimity. Reports of these deeds
revealed an entirely different side of Musolino, and they
resulted in feelings of even more support and approval for
him among southern Italians. Add to this the stories of his
daring public appearances and narrow escapes from those
pursuing him, and it's easy to see why he became such a
prominent figure in the news.

Identifying just when these acts occurred has always
been difficult. Suffice to say that the anecdotes that follow

were all said to have transpired between January 9, 1899 and October 9, 1901, the day he was finally captured.

## Acts of Benevolence

One morning while walking in a wooded area near Brancaleone, a seaside village located some 30 miles from Santo Stefano, Musolino encountered a well-to-do nobleman who at once recognized him from the pictures he had seen in the papers. "Shaking with terror, he laid his purse, containing some five thousand lira, his watch, and his jewelry down on the grass at the feet at the ever dreaded 'brigand.' Musolino looked at him for a moment. He burst out laughing. Then, very soberly, he said: 'Marchese X----makes a mistake. I am still an avenger, not yet a robber.' He took up the valuables, counted the money, returned everything scrupulously, put the Marchese's watch into its owner's pocket for him, and then added five lira to the sum. "For your struggling family, Marchese," he remarked politely, and was out of sight in a moment." [28]

Once when walking in the hills Musolino encountered a peasant weeping. "What has happened to you?" he asked. The poor man was a drover who, after selling his livestock at a cattle fair that day, had been robbed "by Musolino" of all the money he had made. The man went on to describe the highwayman who had stolen his money, and who had boasted that he was the great and terrible bandit. "We will go find *this* Musolino," and sure enough, eventually they did. The real Musolino took out his revolver and forced the imposter to kneel down before the drover, confess his true identity and return the money. He then snatched the drover's whip and vigorously thrashed the stunned robber.

"Now be off!...and remember that Giuseppe Musolino never steals!" The drover looked on in amazement as he realized it was in fact the famous fugitive holding the whip.[29]

In fact, a lot of bandits were exploiting the fear instilled by the name of Musolino. He tracked down another pretender that had robbed a tavern using his name, dragged him back before the owner and forced him to return the money. He then cut off the man's ear, tipped his hat to the astonished landlord, and left.

He once helped a woman chop wood, giving her his scarf when she complained of the cold.

He gave money to a priest for a new church roof.

He provided funds for a poor boy's medical care.

He sewed up a youth's torn clothes.

He performed surgery on two goats to keep them alive for their shepherd owner.

*The Times of London* reported that "...he has shown a sort of Robin Hood spirit of disinterested charity towards the destitute and afflicted; but, unless report does him injustice, his career as Good Samaritan has been far less vigorous and effective than his career as brigand." [30]

## *Acts of Daring*

Musolino's actions also showed him to be courageous, if at times foolhardy. He once dressed himself as a woman and showed up at the death bed of his aunt Filastò, who had given him shelter before he was first arrested, and he is known to have carried a lock of her hair with him from that day forward.

He would run the greatest risks to attend mass. [31] Once he was reportedly seen sitting in church in the same pew as Captain Viola, the commander of the hundreds of Carabinieri troops sent against him.

While he was visiting a mountain town having only one road in and out, he became aware of a column of troops coming towards him in the distance. Surmising that someone must have alerted them to his presence, he quickly slipped into a church, donned a priest's robe and hat he found in a closet, and boldly stole a horse tethered nearby. He slowly rode off down the road and both he and the soldiers stopped when they met. He said he was on his way to see his bishop about some church business, and in an offhanded manner complained about the life of a country priest. After offering their captain some cigars and snuff, he continued on his way – but not before blessing the troops.[32]

Another time soldiers were searching for Musolino in a dense section of forest. They didn't find him, but the day after their search Musolino wrote this letter to the officer in charge:

> "Sir, I cannot compliment the behavior of your soldiers. I reviewed them yesterday from a tree where I was comfortably seated, and am mortified to inform you that they were looking all the time fixedly at the ground, and so did not see me and salute me.
>
> –Yours truly, Giuseppe Musolino."[33]

His father having operated a wine shop, Musolino knew something about the various regional vintages. Once while riding on a train he walked through several of the cars offering samples out of a bottle. Just before he exited the train while it was stopped at a station, he gave the last sample to a passenger near the door. He said he would be glad to sell him a bottle or two if he would only contact him, whereupon he handed him a card. As he watched the supposed wine merchant disappear into the station, the man turned over the card to find Musolino's hand-written name.

"So he went on through summer and winter, protected by fear or favor, frequenting villages and cities of the district, travelling on the railway, entertained in convents or by respectable families, watching from close at hand the progress of bands of police sent out to find him, and then retiring to sleep peacefully in the beds left warm by his early-risen pursuers." [34]

# An Audience with the King

*"The pleasure of roasting Zoccoli and his wife and children alive will yet be mine."*

-Giuseppe Musolino, as quoted in
*The Washington Post*, August 18, 1901

THIS IS JUST ONE CHILLING QUOTE from a famous interview Musolino gave to a reporter on assignment for *The Washington Post*. It was conducted in the outlaw's "mountain stronghold" on July 26, 1901 by Dr. Gaetano Ruffo. Ruffo was also a lawyer who had, through much persistence and patience, managed to arrange the meeting.*
It was a risky undertaking, for he would be at the complete mercy of Italy's most unpredictable and murderous outlaw.

Ruffo had been ordered to wait one morning at a certain point on the road between the towns of Rosarno and Polistena, and to look for a man wearing a white feather

---

*Ruffo was apparently won over to the bandit's cause by this interview, as he would become one of Musolino's defense lawyers at the 1902 trial in Lucca.

in his hat. The man came into sight, but a second man was also seen lurking not far off. This made Ruffo ill at ease.

"Your arms, signor," said the man as he eyed Ruffo intensely, while the other individual positioned himself behind the reporter, who quickly surrendered his knife.

"Better turn your pockets out and loosen your belt," said the man with the feather as he ushered Ruffo into some bushes on the roadside. He said that the interview was not going to happen as originally planned, "But if you come back at 5, I will take you to him without fail."

The journalist gave him an unconvinced look. "Without fail. Signor Musolino himself authorized me to make the promise, and he never breaks his word to friend or enemy."

Ruffo noted that as he walked back to town the second man was following him, and continued to do so until he returned at 5 to the designated spot. The other man was waiting there and the three immediately began walking toward a nearby mountain. Every two miles or so they stopped and Ruffo was left alone while the others scouted out the trail ahead, the reporter having been told not to speak to anyone he encountered if he valued his life. Several times his guide climbed trees for better observation, often making "strange sounds in imitation of birds and animal voices." The anxious reporter deduced these were calls to other confederates to ensure the area was clear of the Carabinieri.

After a while they reached a large clearing which revealed fields planted with crops and fruit trees that were surrounded by hedges. Ruffo would later learn that these were part of an estate belonging to the aristocratic Bomero family.

Without warning a man in ragged clothes popped up from behind a hedge and aimed a double barreled shotgun at them. "His form was clumsy, undersized, and awkward, but his actions betrayed force and agility."

"Halt!" barked the rifleman. One of the escorts gave the password and the man lowered his weapon and became friendly. He raised his cap to Ruffo and said, "I am sorry to ask you to climb over the outer wall of our little fortress." With the help of his guide Ruffo bounded over the hedge and found himself on a slope amid a nursery containing many small olive trees, mingled with mountain wildflowers. He saw three men in front of him: two were standing, rifles in hand, but Musolino remained seated, as if he were a sovereign holding an audience. For the moment, at least, he truly was the King of the Mountains. Ruffo recognized him at once from the many pictures of him he had seen throughout Calabria. But before he could say anything his guide held out his hand and said "My hundred francs, here is Musolino."

After the guide had been paid Musolino began to speak to the journalist in the dialect spoken in Santo Stefano, and each man eyed the other intently. When he caught Ruffo staring at a mole on his left cheek he said, "This is my birthmark, put there so police and military may the easier identify me. God is good to the spies, don't you think so?" The other men standing around laughed heartily.

"But what do you want here? Have you come to persuade me to give myself up?"

"No, only to see, only to speak to you, to enable me to tell the truth about you."

The reporter thought the bandit was dressed as if he were a character in a comic opera; dark velvet suit, red scarf around his neck, a vest bedecked with mostly unidentifiable medals and trinkets, although Ruffo recognized some of them as religious decorations "earned by ardent attendance at church and by charitable acts." A cartridge belt filled with bullets was wrapped around Musolino's waist, and a rifle of exquisite workmanship rested between his knees. A large unsheathed knife hung at his left side together with a gold-plated Navy revolver, confirming reports that the outlaw was left-handed. A pair of binoculars hung from his neck by a leather strap, and "completed his sensational, but at the same time, business-like equipment." As he took out his notepad to begin recording the interview, Ruffo told Musolino he was not only a newspaper man, but also a lawyer.

"I didn't know you were a lawyer as well," replied Musolino. "Being a lawyer you will appreciate the soundness of my defense. I assure you I am the victim of lying tongues – my sentence was a miscarriage of justice. At the hour when that dog Vincenzo Zoccoli was shot I was in bed and asleep. What have you got to say to this, you, from a lawyer's standpoint?"

Ruffo proceeded to explain that from a legal standpoint his defense was not all that sound. Testimony had been given at the trial establishing that Musolino was known to have had a fight with Zoccoli just before the latter was shot. Although they did not see him, witnesses swore they heard Musolino's voice at the scene of the crime, and that his hat and revolver were found nearby. Musolino acknowledged the fight, but then countered each of the other allegations with a detailed account of the flawed logic in them. Ruffo remained unconvinced but didn't say so, as "Musolino's notions of hospitality are too uncertain."

"Is there any truth in the report that you intend to emigrate and leave the country forever?"

"No...my enemies want to make out that I am afraid—I—Musolino, against whom the King sent a whole brigade of soldiers to 'capture or destroy.'" Musolino went on to chronicle many instances of how he had eluded the Carabinieri, and how he had never feared them because he possessed the support of the people. He asserted that the reason the troops were finally recalled was due to his having written several letters to the Minister of War, in which he pointed out the futility of maintaining the chase. "I have no ambition to subject my fellow citizens to needless expense," he wrote. "Your men have searched every thicket, every cave, every field and forest, every castle, every town, house, and hut in the territory I call my own; they cannot, or will not, find me – why persist in measures that cover Italian arms with ridicule?"

Musolino then stood up and began vigorously stamping his feet, declaring that his initiative had saved the government three to four million francs, but that his thanks was only to have the Minister of Justice raise the reward from his capture, dead or alive, to 50,000 francs.* "A whole army corps couldn't scare me, but those 50,000 franc's reward is quite another matter...The hope of getting so much money may turn even an honest man into an assassin. I see my finish."

Ruffo proposed that Musolino might be able to claim the money himself if he gave himself up, contingent on the promise of a new trial. "True," replied the bandit, but went on to say that while he would fully expect the original false

---

* roughly the purchasing power of over $200,000 today

verdict to be overturned, he had since committed other acts that would be seen as crimes, and that he would need a guarantee of exemption from prosecution, "before I can even think of giving myself up."

Ruffo said that he knew the mayor of Santo Stefano had recently journeyed to Rome and made this very proposal for immunity to officials at the Ministry of Justice on Musolino's behalf.

"Precisely…Have you heard whether he was favorably received by the authorities?"

"I met him in Rome as he was coming from the Palace of Justice."

"And the result? Speak, man!"

"The minister refused to entertain the proposition, I am sorry to say."

Ruffo again proposed that Musolino give himself up, contending that an open-minded jury would decide his fate, not the government. "I have no more faith in juries than in judges, for both can be bought or terrorized. Only a full pardon, signed by the Kings [*sic*] own hand, can lure me from these mountains." He clarified that the pardon need only be for the crimes committed after the first Zoccoli incident, and that he would be willing to again stand trial on the original charge if guaranteed an unprejudiced jury. He was convinced he would be acquitted. He asked Ruffo if he would draft the necessary document to send to the King, promising to pay him 10,000 francs from the reward money he would receive. Ruffo nervously declined.

Musolino then asked if the lawyer knew of any way to ensure a sympathetic jury. The brigand was known to be epileptic, and Ruffo opined that some people had gotten off by pleading epilepsy, explaining that "a criminal might secure a berth in an insane asylum by feigning irresponsibility on account of physical or mental disease…from the insane asylum to complete liberty is but a step."

Musolino became white with rage. "You seem to forget you are talking to an innocent man…I am not going to play the bedlamite for the Roman cabinet's benefit! No! Three times no! None of your justice for me! I shall continue to be my own law-giver. Here's my symbol of justice!"

Ruffo stood petrified and didn't know what would happen next. Musolino tossed his rifle in the air, grabbed it as it came down, and took aim. "None of your justice. I had a taste of it once and it stinks," he said. "His face became terribly distorted, like that of an animal ready to spring on his prey."

"Blood is the order of the day. I want to see blood," Musolino yelled as the reporter beheld the unfolding of a scene bordering on the surreal. Musolino took out his knife, tossed it in the air catching it between his teeth, raised his rifle with his right hand and leveled his revolver with his left. "I have never been a lamb, but am more of a tiger than ever now."

Musolino then told Ruffo that his next victims would be a man named Zirollo and one of the bandit's own cousins whom he knew had spoken to the police. "As for that precious relative of mine, I will make him die by inches. A fellow who betrays his own kin deserves nothing better."

"I thought you loved your relatives."

"I do, Ruffo, I do. Haven't I murdered a governor who incarcerated my girl cousin?"

"But are you sure of Vittoreo's treachery?"

"He and his partner are as guilty as Marte was."

Musolino then explained in detail how he happened

to kill Marte, as described in an earlier chapter. The chilling blow-by-blow account of the cold-blooded murder left Ruffo terribly shaken, yet he somehow managed not to show any emotion. After "an uncomfortable pause," he continued with the interview.

"You claim that all your deeds are excusable on the ground that you merely punish personal enemies who thought to destroy you by false testimony, or by earning the rewards set upon your head."

"Correctly spoken, Mr. Lawyer," said Musolino approvingly, as he immediately launched into a description of how he had killed a man named Chirico who had testified against him. He had hunted him down only two days after his escape from prison, catching up with him while Chirico was walking with his young son on a mountainside. The boy begged Musolino to have pity on his father. After telling him that he would, the bandit told the boy to run home.

"And instead of torturing Chirico, as he had richly deserved, I killed him by a single shot through the heart. Yet they call me cruel, Ruffo."

"I am told Vincenzo Zoccoli will not appear against you a second time if you submit and brave another trial."

"I know he won't for he must die before I consent to place myself once more at the mercy of our judicial system."

After hearing this Ruffo, in shock, let out an involuntary sigh. After a pause, Musolino shrugged his shoulders and said, "You are only a lawyer and a newspaper man, you don't understand." He went on to describe how he had sought to kill Vincenzo on multiple occasions, two that were nearly successful, but had managed only to kill Vincenzo's brother Henrico. With a horrifyingly relaxed attitude Musolino described how he had first shot the man in the leg before carving him up with his knife.

"Ah, how I wallowed in his blood. If I had owned a tub I would have taken a bath in it. I tell you Ruffo, if you want a real elixir of life, drink the blood of your enemies. There is nothing like it."

Musolino then gave multiple accounts of other murders committed during the past year, sparing none of the grisly details. Finally Ruffo could take no more, and after much prodding he got Musolino to start talking about his dealings with the Carabinieri and the police.

"We are very good friends…even though I have sometimes been obliged to shoot one or the other who got too fresh; I am sure no trooper sent against me will ever attempt to capture me. I have often played cards with the King's soldiers who, of course, affected not to know me. And once or twice I attended church together with the commanding general and his staff. He, too, was conveniently blind. Tell this to the newspapers, it will amuse the people."

Musolino then asked if the newspapers still carried as much news about him as when his vendetta first began. When Ruffo answered yes, he seemed so pleased that the reporter summoned up the courage to ask him about his family.

"Many good people blame you for allowing your parents and other relatives to languish in jail on your account."

"On my account?" screamed Musolino. Am I the government, pray? The imprisonment of my old father, mother, and sister is nothing short of blackmail on the part of the state, which thinks the desire to help my loved ones will drive me to surrender. But the Musolinos are a hardy race – they will endure anything rather than dishonor. No, and if my whole family should die and rot in prison, I shall never submit to injustice; moreover my folks don't ask the sacrifice of me – they wouldn't accept it."

"But surrounded by spies as you are, are you not afraid that possibly you may fall into the hands of your enemies alive? In that case, nothing can save you from a life sentence."

"Nothing but this," said Musolino as he held up a little bottle reputed to contain strychnine, "and this," holding out his two quivering hands. At this time the guide stepped forward and suggested that it was getting late and that he and Ruffo should head back down the mountain. Musolino then walked over to Ruffo, and after grasping his hand said, "I have been thinking, there is still another way out of the difficulty. The people must elect me to Parliament; then the King will have to grant me an unconditional pardon, as he did in the case of Felice. Consider this proposal, Ruffo! As a deputy I can snap my fingers at the courts and may even be persuaded to forgive my enemies.

Ruffo pointed out that while the socialist De Felice had been condemned to 20 years imprisonment for political crimes and was later elected to Parliament and eventually pardoned, he hadn't killed anyone.

"And I am not a criminal, either…how often shall I proclaim my innocence?" roared Musolino so loudly that a small bird in a tree above was frightened and flew away.

"Never mind, he will come back, for he has his nest here. Ah, everybody has a home – everybody but Musolino, who must slink from mountain to valley, from forest to fields without rest, without peace until lightening strikes him to the ground." He shook Ruffo's hand once more, saying, "If you hear I am dead, pray for me…pray for me and tell all the world that Musolino was an honest man."

"But remember, Ruffo, I won't die in a hurry. Saint Joseph has lately consented to become my special protector, for he knows I am innocent of the crime that drove me to this."

Ruffo took his leave and went back down the mountain to write his story, the article being simultaneously published in Italy's *Il Secolo Illustrato* (Milan) and *The Washington Post*. Musolino had not yet reached the height of his notoriety, and he now had a huge transatlantic audience eagerly awaiting news of his next move.

# A Bid for Freedom, Then Capture

> *"Fate, show thy force; ourselves we do not owe;*
> *What is decreed must be; and be this so"*

-William Shakespeare, Twelfth Night

ALTHOUGH THERE HAD BEEN SCORES of failed attempts to capture Musolino, the noose was beginning to tighten around him. Up to 200 of his relatives and acquaintances were now in jail, gathered there by the regime to pressure him to give himself up. The reward for his capture had also been increased, and in desperation the government told the Carabinieri and police to intensify their hunt. They launched an unprecedented expansion of checkpoints at transportation hubs throughout Calabria and immediate searches of anybody who they thought had information about Musolino. This was in addition to their ongoing patrols in the mountains and forests of Aspromonte.

Musolino one day received a rather curious proposition from the government. A private ship would be sent to meet him at the dock at Cape Bruzzano, just outside the town of Africo. The ship would take him to France where he would then be free to immigrate to America if he wished. The reason given by the government was simply that they wanted to be rid of him; the unprecedented embarrassment and expense his pursuit had caused the country could not continue. Musolino was of course suspicious of this proposal, but he was now desperate and willing to gamble. After his supporters informed him that a ship was in fact sent to the designated location, he made his way to the cape. His luck had not run out just yet, as Musolino somehow discovered it was a trap. He turned back only a short time before he would have presented himself at the pier for boarding.

There are confusing accounts in several Italian sources about a Carabinieri scheme to lure Musolino to a meal of hot pasta brought to him one night by a turncoat brigand named Prince. The pasta sauce was to have been mixed with some opium paste, so that after the meal the sleepy bandit could easily be subdued by a contingent of troops lurking nearby. As it was, the opium had little or no effect on Musolino. Prince managed to slip away, walking some distance to where the police were waiting. The officer in charge directed Prince to return to Musolino, and, when the two were together, light a cigar. Their exact position would thus be identified and the troops would quietly close in around them. Sometime after 1 a.m. Prince lit his cigar, but then he panicked and immediately dropped to the ground. One of the Carabinieri ignored orders and broke the silence, shouting, "Who goes there?" Musolino, realizing he had been betrayed, took out his revolver and shot Prince three times.[35] The police approached the spot cautiously, not knowing how many guns might now be pointed at them. By the time they reached Prince's body, Musolino was already some distance away.

After a time he encountered a single Carabiniere. "I am Musolino…let me pass." The startled soldier attempted to fire his rifle, but Musolino fired first. Although he maintained he was trying to only wound the man in the leg, the shot proved fatal. For the rest of his life, Musolino maintained this was the only innocent person he had ever killed, made necessary by the regrettable circumstances under which the two had met.[36]

On July 29, 1900, King Umberto I of Italy was assassinated by an anarchist named Gaetano Bresci. The act was in revenge for the ruthless suppression of a workers' protest in Milan which left hundreds dead. Umberto was succeeded by his son, King Victor Emmanuel III, and Musolino had heard that the new King was a different man than his father, who had never replied to several letters the outlaw had sent him urging political and economic reforms in the south. Some sources say Musolino decided to make the 300 mile journey to Rome to arrange an audience with Victor Emmanuel, but others say passage on a ship had been arranged which would take him from Genoa to America. Musolino believed that efforts to capture him would not be nearly as thorough at the great port located over 600 miles from where he was thought to be roaming.

Musolino said his farewells and set out on his long journey alone, intending to take a route up the center of Italy, so he could remain in the sparsely populated Apennine mountains most of the way. Then, on the 9th of October, 1901, Musolino's great spree of crime, benevolence, and daring came to a sudden end. He fell into the hands of the Carabinieri: literally.

While walking north approaching the town of Urbino, hundreds of miles from where he had started his trek, he observed two Carabinieri, Antonio La Serra and Amerigo Feliziani di Baschi, walking towards him.[37] Musolino had no way of knowing that they were searching for someone else who had murdered a policeman in the area, and that he himself was not suspected to be the vicinity. After spotting them from a distance, Musolino turned around and began walking swiftly towards some woods. The soldiers still didn't know who he was or why he was departing so quickly, but now they suspected he might be the killer they were seeking. La Serra was recovering from an injury and could not keep up with di Baschi, who hurried after Musolino. When the two came face to face Musolino affected an aura of complete indifference, and attempted to walk past the official. He was ordered to stop. The startled look in the bandit's eyes caused di Baschi to believe he had found the murderer they had been trying to find, and when Musolino started sprinting away, he gave chase as the brigand darted into a nearby vineyard.

Musolino was the faster of the two and was beginning to outdistance his pursuer when he suddenly tripped over a strand of wire stretched among the vines. Musolino grabbed his revolver but before he could get up di Baschi dove on top of him. As the two were wrestling La Serra finally caught up with them, and after a vigorous struggle the two Carabinieri proved too much for Musolino. According to di Baschi he offered them 250 lira in exchange for his freedom,[38] as they were still unaware of his identity. They refused the offer, put him in handcuffs, and escorted him to the jail at Urbino. Not long after his capture a saying became popular throughout Italy: *"Quello in cui ha fallito un esercito, c'è riuscito un filo* (where an army failed, a wire succeeded)."

Suddenly the most extensive manhunt in Italian history was over, and it seemed somewhat anticlimactic, given the expectation by many that the nearly three-year chase would end in a deadly volley of gunfire. However, it was no sure thing that this was the end for Musolino, since it was doubtful if any jury in Calabria could be found that would convict him, no matter the evidence. The bandit had become so famous that prominent lawyers from all over Italy sought to be on his defense team. Soon after Musolino was arrested, the noted Italian poet Giovanni Pascoli said he respected the bandit's "sovereign intelligence" and dedicated an ode to him entitled *Musolino incompiuta* (Musolino Unfinished.)

The first show-trial of a united Italy was about to begin.

Giuseppe Musolino, *Il Brigante* (The Brigand) shortly after his capture in 1901.

"After the three men shot Marte, Musolino finished him off with his long knife." 1914 drawing by Carlo Chiostri, who also illustrated the first edition of *Pinocchio*.

Musolino and his confederates exchange gunfire with
government troops sent into the mountains to capture
them. (Carlo Chiostri)

Musolino captured near Urbino after tripping over a wire.
From Domenica del Corriere, Milan, October, 1901

Musolino and his accomplices in the
courtroom dock in Lucca. (Illustrated London
News, May 5, 1902)

Musolino refuses to go to the courtroom unless he can
appear in his own clothes. (drawing by Carlo Chiostri)

The crack legal team representing Musolino and his
accomplices at the Lucca trial. Gaetano Ruffo, who
once interviewed the outlaw for the *Washington
Post*, is third from top left. From a postcard sold in
Lucca during the trial.

Scene from the Lucca trial which shows Musolino seated on
the bottom bench of the dock. This illustration appeared in La
Domenica del Corriere, 4 May, 1902.

Poster for the 1931 silent film "Giuseppe Musolino,"
which played to packed houses in cities in the United
States with large Italian-American populations. No
copies are known to have survived, but the New York
State Archives has a copy of the script.

Colorful paperback books about Musolino's exploits were extremely
popular throughout Italy between 1902 and the 1950's.

# The Great Trial at Lucca

*"He is the most remarkable being that has ever stood behind the bars of Italian justice."*

-*The New York Times* referring to Musolino,
June 22, 1902

NEWS OF MUSOLINO'S CAPTURE blanketed front pages of newspapers throughout Italy and around the world. "Capture of Man of Many Crimes," read the *Boston Daily Globe*, [41] and the *New York Times* [40] proclaimed "Italian Brigand Musolino Captured."

The government was right to be concerned that any jury selected in Reggio di Calabria, the provincial capital, would be intensely biased in Musolino's favor. They were also worried they wouldn't be able to hold onto him. "There is an almost universal belief that Musolino will not have to wait to be condemned, but will escape through the connivance of sympathizers." [41]

If he were acquitted, the government would face further humiliation and ridicule beyond that which had resulted by the scope and lengthy duration of the manhunt.

The Minister of Justice therefore decided to transfer the trial to the Corte d'Assise in the Tuscan city of Lucca. Some logistical problems would be incurred to transport the required witnesses for both the prosecution and the defense to Lucca from Calabria, over 600 miles distant, as well as to house and feed them while they were waiting to appear in court. No matter, it was deemed imperative that Musolino not be tried in a location where he had the backing of the great majority of the population. The criminal justice system may not have gotten things right in his first trial, but efforts would be made to ensure Musolino's second one would be by the book.

The world's interest in the trial was said to be only slightly less than that which existed during the famous second trial of France's Captain Alfred Dreyfus in 1899. [42] Every leading newspaper in Italy was represented in the courtroom, as well as many foreign papers. Musolino was now only 27 years old and "altogether of an attractive appearance," [43] although he took great umbrage when he saw artists drawing him in the courtroom. He usually scowled at them and turned his back.

Musolino's main defense was that he was a well-documented epileptic, and this condition, when combined with the impact of the injustice that had been done to him during his previous trial, had impaired his ability to temper his actions. [44] His lawyers maintained that Musolino had never killed anybody who had either not falsely testified against him or fired on him first. They argued that "he has exercised the sacred right of avenging himself on enemies." [45]

On the first day of the trial Musolino initially refused to leave his cell and go to the packed courtroom, with scores of more people lined up outside hoping to just to get a glimpse of him. He had been issued ill-fitting striped prison garb and maintained that, since he had not yet been convicted of the charges now brought against him, he should be allowed to wear his own clothes. After a while he relented and went to the courtroom, but the issue came up soon after proceedings had begun:

MUSOLINO: "I am a gentleman, not a malefactor."

JUDGE: "You will be judged by your words, not by your clothes."

MUSOLINO: "Not a bit. Who'd listen to you here if you were dressed like a goat herd?"

JUDGE: "Then I must question you as you are. Did you kill Sidari?"

MUSOLINO: "Yes!"

JUDGE: "Why?"

MUSOLINO: "I won't speak!"

JUDGE: "You must!"

MUSOLINO: "I won't til I have my own clothes."

JUDGE: "You must! Have you or have you not killed?"

MUSOLINO: "You want me to speak and I tell you I won't speak!"

This bit of theater went on for some time until finally the judge ordered a recess, and Musolino's lawyers used the time to convince him he should speak. When the court reconvened Musolino launched into a comprehensive accounting of his crimes, complete with full-bodied dialogue, elaborate gestures, and tears. Gradually a role reversal of sorts occurred and Musolino began interrupting the proceedings and was "immediately listened to in a death-like silence, and his remarks are followed with thunders of applause, and sometimes by hysterical weeping." [46] He acted truly penitent when he talked about the only member of the Carabinieri he had ever slain, but said he had no choice because the officer fired on him first.

On trial were also three other men charged as accomplices: Rocco Perpiglia, age 19; Stefano De Lorenzo, age 27; and Giovanni Jati, age 25. [47] All the men were defended by a team of ten influential and ambitious lawyers. All went smoothly for some weeks until one of the lawyers was interviewed by a reporter. The attorney described how each member of the team was responsible for a specific aspect of the case, but that he was overall the person in charge. When the other lawyers read the published interview, they all became indignant and resigned. The judge threatened to hold them in contempt of court and they quickly resumed their work, but they soon resigned again over one of the judge's procedural rulings against them. This time they did not come back. Several other lawyers were requested to defend Musolino but they all refused, probably because the case was by now seen as going against the defendant. Musolino had demonstrated from the dock what a charismatic and clever person he was, and few thought his claim that epilepsy had led him to commit his bloody rampage would prove successful. "Finally, an old lawyer, eighty-three years of age, accepted the charge." [48]

During the trial Musolino received thousands of letters and telegrams expressing sympathy, "of which he is monstrously proud." One letter published in Italian newspapers and signed by "a hundred women of decent position in Florence," said the women prayed for Musolino's acquittal and hoped to meet him upon his release.[49]

While Musolino was in detention two eminent psychiatrists, Professor Enrico Morselli and Dr. Santé De Sanctis, were given permission to conduct a thorough physical and psychological examination of him. They compiled a precise record of multiple aspects of his body measurements, took his fingerprints, recorded his body temperature and blood pressure over time, calculated his reflexes, and listed the topics of his nightly dreams. Their findings were published in a book of over 400 pages in 1903.[50] They concluded that Musolino was, physiologically and psychologically, normal.[51]

After a trial of two months duration the jury pronounced Musolino guilty on all 37[52] charges. The judge sentenced him to life imprisonment with the first eight years in solitary confinement.* It was well-understood that most prisoners would go mad before such a lengthy stay in solitary was completed. The state may not be able to take Musolino's life, but they could try to take away his sanity. The psychiatrists who had examined Musolino during the trial commented that such a lengthy sentence of solitary confinement was "a shame to our penal and prison legislation, for it involves a physical and moral

---

*Italy had no death penalty at the time. Some sources say the first 10 years were to be in solitary.

torture far more atrocious than instantaneous death at the hands of the hangman." [53]

When the sentence was pronounced in the name of King Victor Emmanuel III, Musolino stood and delivered the following reply: "Within a year I shall be free. The king does not count. The people are everything and the people are for me. If I shall not be set free, there will be a republic of blood. I am calm because I believe in God." [54]

Then Musolino pleaded very persuasively for clemency for his three comrades who had not yet heard their sentences. "With tears in his eyes Musolino assured the jury of the innocence of his comrades and begged for their acquittal. The court and jury were visibly affected by Musolino's eloquence, and the other prisoners were discharged." [55]

Musolino was to serve his sentence on Elba, the same island to which the Emperor Napoleon had been exiled before he escaped to fight his last great battle at Waterloo. He was transferred by boat to the prison fortress of San Giacomo at Portolongone*, where his accommodations and food would be far below the standard which Napoleon had enjoyed. Musolino was placed in a cell with nothing but a single mattress on the floor. The cells on either side as well as above and below him were to be kept vacant at all times, except at night when the one above was occupied by a jailer, who could never be from Calabria. Human contact was to be kept to an absolute minimum. He was fed mostly a diet of thick soup, and his correspondence was severely restricted: he could receive one letter every four months, and send only one during that same period. He

*Present-day Porto Azzurro

was occasionally allowed to see visitors, which included some very distinguished ones

Gradually these conditions produced the intended effect. In August of 1907 the *New York Times* wrote, "Three years ago he was quite himself, courteous and vivacious and using ornate phrases and magnificent gestures. Since then he has gradually deteriorated, and it seems that nothing can save him." [57]

Sadly, we don't know if Musolino was ever told – or if he was, if he understood – that in 1933 a letter had been published in Italy which purported to exonerate him of the original charge of attempted murder against Vincenzo Zoccoli. A man named Giuseppe Travia, who had immigrated to America and was one of Musolino's acquaintances in the tavern the day of the knife fight with Zoccoli, admitted that he was the unseen man who had fired from behind a wall. Although this confession had no impact on his sentence, at last there was evidence to corroborate Musolino's claim of innocence to the charge that had first started him on the road to fame and ruin.

# Il Finale

"*The southern imagination at once took hold of his adventurous career, embellished it with romance and threw around it a glamour which makes him even now, while in prison serving a life-term fixed by his recent conviction, a hero, a demigod and a martyr.*"

- *The Washington Bee*, August 30, 1902

MUSOLINO WAS THOUGHT TO BE GOING MAD as early as 1907, but it wasn't until 1946 that he was officially declared insane and transferred to the asylum in Reggio di Calabria. The *New York Times* noted that Musolino "was the terror of southern Italy thirty years ago." [58] He would spend the final ten years of his life here, and at least it would be under more comfortable conditions. Even now, in his 70's, his charisma was still evident. "With patience and persistence, he wrangled the director's permission to take short walks around the city. Every Monday, rain or shine, Musolino drew crowds of onlookers." [59]

One day after these outings had become routine, the nurse who was escorting the aged outlaw around the city decided to take him to her house so the two could enjoy a home-cooked lunch. Afterwards the two fell asleep, or so it seemed. When the nurse awoke Musolino was nowhere to be seen. The panicky staffer ran out into the street and asked a group of women on their way to do some laundry if they had seen an old man walking about. They answered yes; they had seen someone walking towards the sea. The nurse realized there was a small train station in that direction, and she ran as fast as she could until she reached the tracks. There she spotted Musolino climbing aboard a train, but she managed to yank him off and quickly returned him to the asylum.

Musolino died on Thursday, January 22, 1956, and his body was taken back to his hometown for burial. He was eighty years old. Time magazine noted that, even though he had been in prison or the asylum for over half a century, "Musolino's reputation survives in ballads still sung…As the entire town of Santo Stefano filed silently to the cemetery, black-rimmed posters appeared on village walls all over Calabria saying, 'Musolino is dead. He held liberty high.'" [60]

# Endnotes

[1] "King of the Mountains," *Time*, February 6, 1956, pg. 32.

[2] "High Fascists Released," *New York Times*, June 27, 1946.

[3] Duggan, Christopher. *The Force of Destiny: A History of Italy Since 1796*. New York: Houghton Mifflin, 2008. pg 245-6.

[4] "Musolino the Bandit," H.D. Sedgwick, Jr., *The Outlook*, August 30, 1902, pg. 1059.

[5] Ibid,, pg. 1057.

[6] "Fratelli di sangue," Nicola Gratteri and Antonio Nicaso, Mondadori, *Milan, 2006*.

[7] "The Last Italian Brigand," Salvatore Cortesi, *The Independent*, May 22, 1902, pg. 1241.

[8] "Italian Brigand Musolino Captured," *The New York Times*, October 17, 1901.

[9] "Italy's Famous Bandit," *The Washington Post*, August 18, 1901, pg. 19.

[10] "Calabrian Man Hunt," *The Washington Post*, May 12, 1901, pg 16.

[11] "Italian Brigand Musolino Captured," *The New York Times*, October 17, 1901.

[12] "The Vendetta of Musolino," *The Wide World Magazine*, Vol. VI, No. 33, December 1900, pg. 256.

[13] "The Last Italian Brigand," Salvatore Cortesi, *The Independent*, May 22, 1902, pg. 1241.

[14] "Calabrian Man Hunt," *The Washington Post*, May 12, 1901, pg 16.

[15] "The Last Italian Brigand," Salvatore Cortesi, *The Independent*, May 22, 1902, pg. 1241.

[16] "The Vendetta of Musolino," *The Wide World Magazine*, Vol. VI, No. 33, December 1900, pg. 256.

[17] Ibid.

[18] The Last Italian Brigand," Salvatore Cortesi, *The Independent*, May 22, 1902, pg. 1242.

[19] "Italy's Famous Bandit," *The Washington Post*, August 18, 1901, pg. 19.

[20] Ibid.

[21] "Italy's Famous Bandit," *The Washington Post*, August 18, 1901, pg. 19.

[22] "The Brigand Musolio," *The Times of London*, October 26, 1901, pg. 15.

[23] "The Last Italian Brigand," Salvatore Cortesi, *The Independent*, May 22, 1902, pg. 1242.

[24] "Musolino the Bandit," *The Outlook*, August 30, 1902, pg. 1058.

[25] "The Last Italian Brigand," Salvatore Cortesi, *The Independent*, May 22, 1902, pg. 1242.

[26] Ibid, pg. 1240.

[27] "The Last Italian Brigand," Salvatore Cortesi, *The Independent*, May 22, 1902, pg. 1242.

[28] "An Italian Brigand of To-day," Irenaeus Prime-Stevenson, *The Independent*, August 8, 1901, pg. 1847.

[29] Ibid, pg. 1846

[30] "Musolino the Bandit," H.D. Sedgwick, Jr., *The Outlook*, August 30, 1902, pg. 1060.

[31] "The Brigand Musolino," *The Times of London*, October 26, 1901, pg. 15.

[32] "A Bandit Bold," *West Gippsland Gazette* (Australia)," December 10, 1901.

[33] Ibid.

[34] "Biografia di un Bandito (book review)," *The Nation*, October 29, 1903, pg. 348.

[35] "The Vendetta of Musolino," *The Wide World Magazine*, Vol. VI, No. 33, December 1900, pg. 258.

[36] Ibid.

[37] "Musolino, Il Bandito per Vendetta," Adriano Salani, Florence, 1923, pg. 66. (reprint of 1914 edition)

[38] http://www.centrostudimalfatti.org/old/a_feliziani.html, accessed July 22, 2012.

[39] "Capture of Man of Many Crimes," *Boston Daily Globe*, October 17, 1901

[40] "Italian Brigand Musolino Captured," *New York Times*, October 17, 1901.

[41] *Los Angeles Times*, April 27, 1902

[42] "Musolino's Actions in the Court Room, *The New York Times*, June 22 1902.

[43] Ibid

[44] *Los Angeles Times*, April 27, 1902.

[45] Ibid.

[46] "Audacity of a Brigand," *The Yukon Sun*, Oklahoma Territory, May 22, 1902, pg. 7.

[47] "Musolino, Il Bandito per Vendetta," Adriano Salani, Florence, 1923, pg. 73. (reprint of 1914 edition)

[48] "Musolino the Bandit," H.D. Sedgwick, Jr., *The Outlook*, August 30, 1902, pg. 1058.

[49] Trial of Musolino, *Aukland Star*, June 21, 1902, pg. 5.

[50] "Biografia di un bandito, Giuseppe Musolino," E. Morselli & S. De Sanctis, Fratelli Treves, Milan, 1903.

[51] "Biografia di un bandito, Giuseppe Musolino (book review)," *The Nation*, October 29, 1903, pg. 348.

[52] "Musolino, Il Bandito per Vendetta," Adriano Salani, Florence, 1923, pg. 235. (reprint of 1914 edition)

[53] "Biografia di un bandito, Giuseppe Musolino (book review)," *The Nation*, October 29, 1903, pg. 348.

[54] "Musolino the Bandit," H.D. Sedgwick, Jr., *The Outlook*, August 30, 1902, pg. 1059.

[55] "Musolino's Life Sentence," The *New York Times*, June 12, 1902.

[56] "Bandit Musolino is Going Insane," *New York Times*," August 4, 1907.

[57] Ibid.

[58] "High Fascists Released," *New York Times*, June 27, 1946.

[59] "Booked: The Last 150 Years Told Through Mug Shots," Giacomo Papi, Seven Stories Press, eBook, 2011

[60] "King of the Mountains," *Time*, February 6, 1956, pg. 32.

# About the Author

Dan Possumato is retired from the U.S. Army and holds a M.S. degree from Johns Hopkins University as well as a diploma from the U.S. Army War College. This is his first book, which he extensively researched from contemporary source documents gathered from far-flung and difficult-to-obtain records. His grandfather was Giovanni Musolino, a first cousin of the famous outlaw who, as a boy of ten or eleven, actually met his fugitive relative while he was on the loose. It was from him that he first heard the fantastic stories about *Il Brigante*. He lives in Pittsburgh with his wife, Ellen Steinbart.